Guess What!

Student's Book 1A

Susannah Reed with Kay Bentley
Series Editor: Lesley Koustaff

CAMBRIDGE
UNIVERSITY PRESS

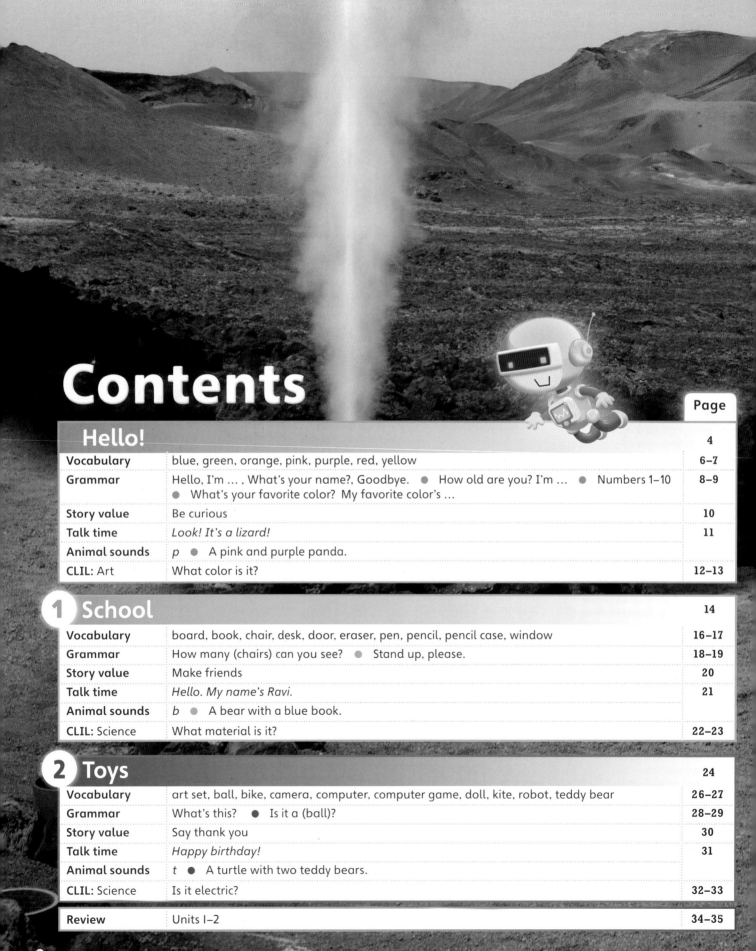

Contents

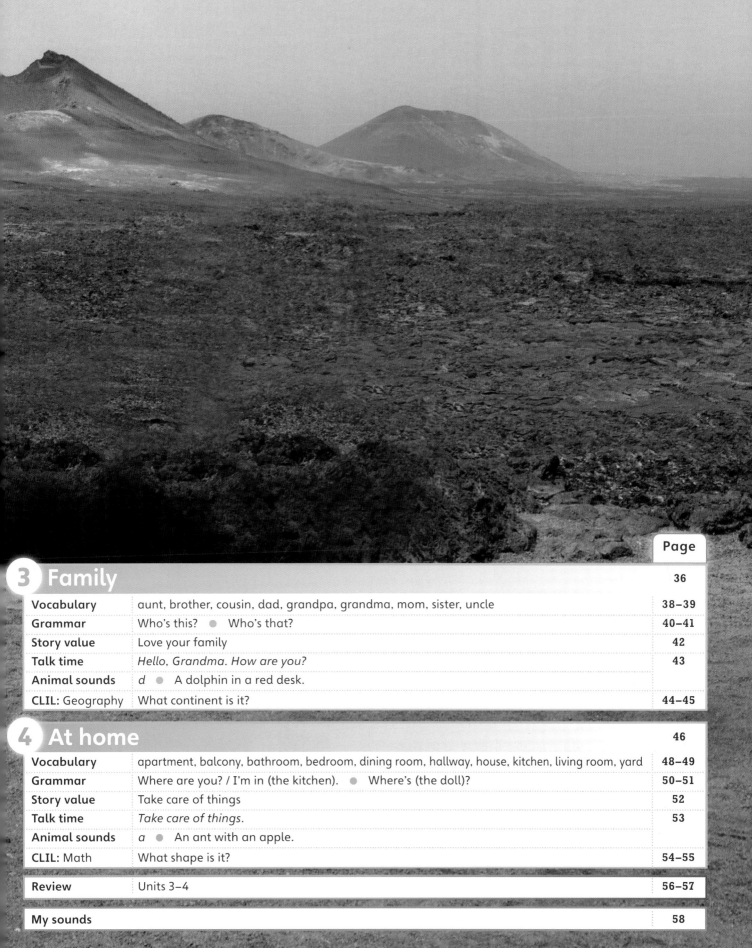

Hello!

Guess What!

1 (CD1 03) **Listen. Who's speaking?**

2 (CD1 04) **Listen, point, and say.**

3 (CD1 05) **Listen and find.**

Find Leo

Say the chant.

5 Think **Look and say the name.**

Number 1. David.

1

3

2

4

Vocabulary **7**

6 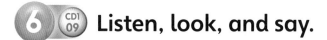 **CD1 09 Listen, look, and say.**

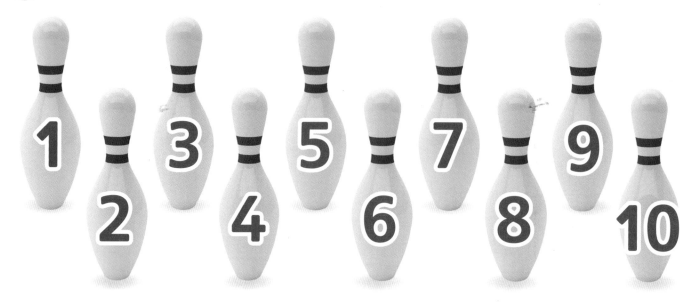

1 2 3 4 5 6 7 8 9 10

7 Look and match.

1 2 3

8 7 6

8 CD1 10 Now listen and check.

9 **Listen, point, and say.**

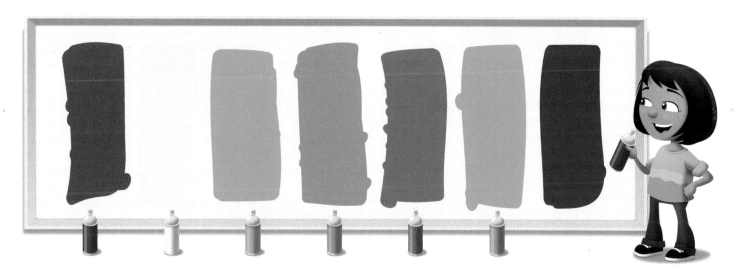

10 (CD1 13) **Sing the song.**

11 (About Me) **Ask and answer.**

How old are you?   I'm six.

What's your favorite color?   My favorite color's blue.

12 CD1 15 **Listen.**

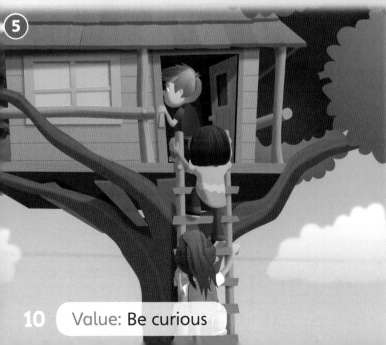

Value: Be curious

→ Workbook page 8

13 (CD1 17) *Talk Time* Listen and act.

Animal sounds

14 (CD1 18) Listen and say.

A pink and purple panda.

What
color is it?

1 (CD1 20) **Listen and say.**

2 **Watch the video.**

3 **Say the color.**

Number 1. Orange.　Yes.

Guess What!

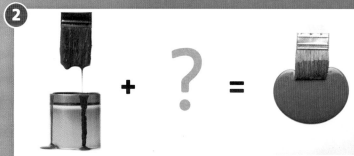

Project

4 **Make a rainbow.**

1 School

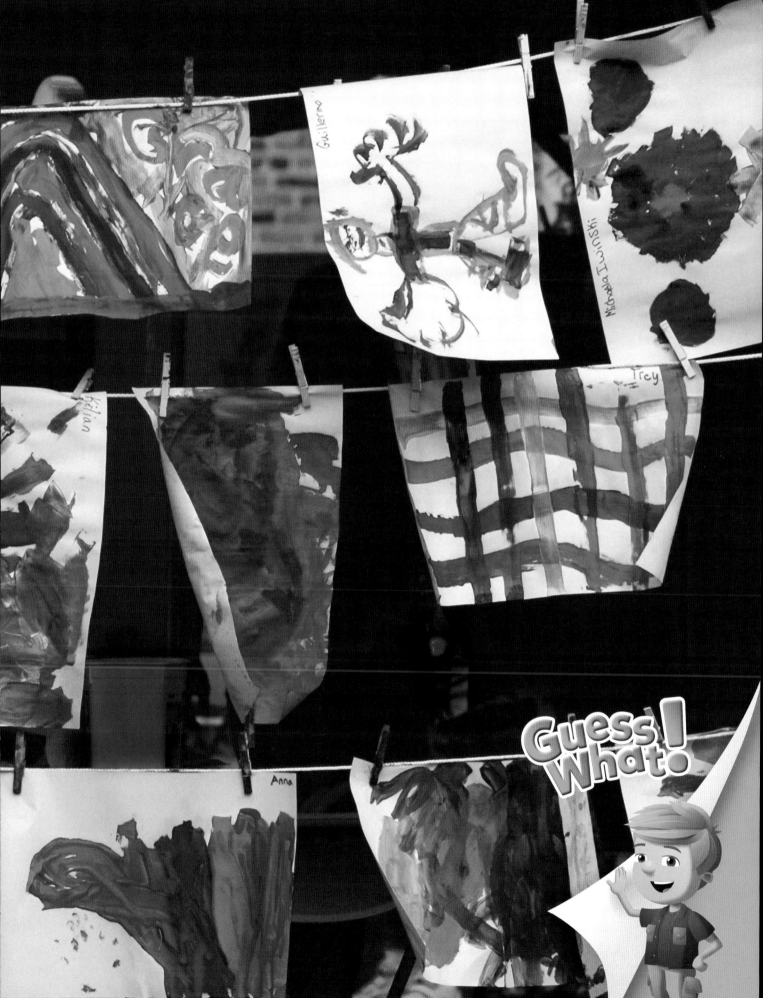

Guess What!

1 CD1 22 Listen. Who's speaking?

2 CD1 23 Listen, point, and say.

3 CD1 24 Listen and find.

Find Leo

4 CD1 26 **Say the chant.**

5 Think **Look and find five differences.**

Picture 1. A purple pen.   Picture 2. A purple pencil.

6 CD1 28 **Sing the song.**

7 CD1 29 **Listen and answer the questions.**

How many chairs can you see?

Six!

1 **2** **3**  **4** **5**

8 CD1 30 **Listen, point, and say.**

9 CD1 31 **Listen and do the action.**

10 **Play the game.**

Open your book.

Grammar: *Stand up, please.* **19**

12 CD1 35 (Talk Time) **Listen and act.**

Animal sounds

13 CD1 36 **Listen and say.**

A bear with a blue book.

What
material
is it?

1 (CD1 38) **Listen and say.**

1

2

3

4
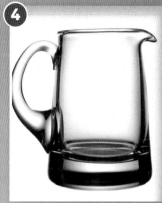

2 **Watch the video.**

3 **Look and say** *wood,* *plastic, metal,* or *glass.*

Number 1. Wood.   Yes.

Guess What!

1

2

3

4

Project

4 **Draw materials in your classroom.**

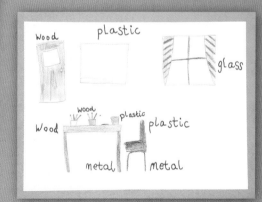

2 Toys

Guess What!

→ Workbook page 20

Say the chant.

 Look and find five missing toys in picture 2.

The yellow ball.

6 CD1 46 **Listen, look, and say.**

7 Think **Look and say.**   What's this?   It's a kite.

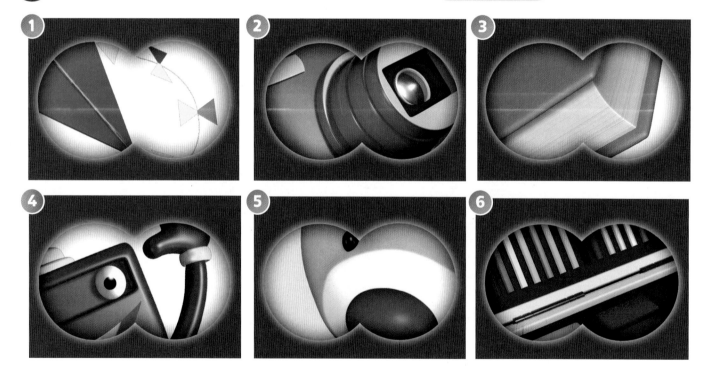

8 CD1 47 **Now listen and check.**

9 CD1 49 **Sing the song.**

10 **Play the game.**

Is it a ball?

No, it isn't.

Grammar: *Is it a ball?* **29**

12   Listen and act.

Animal sounds

13 Listen and say.

A **t**urtle with
two **t**eddy bears.

Is it electric?

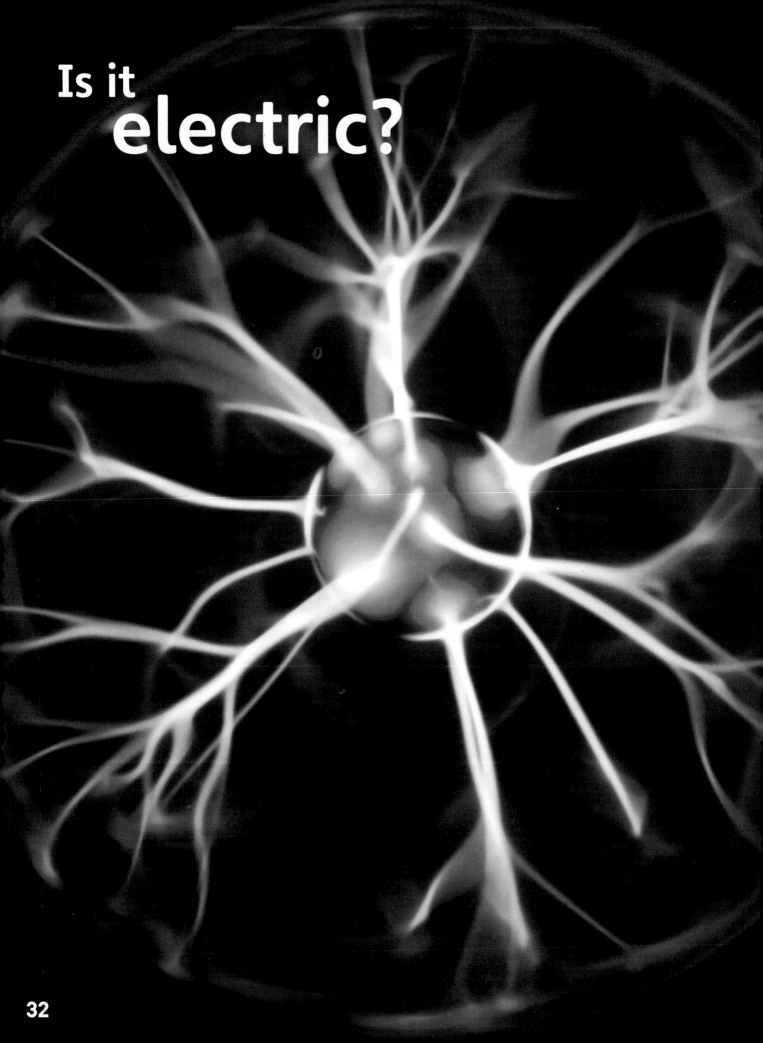

1  Listen and say.

1

2

3

2 Watch the video.

3 Look and say *it's electric*, or *it isn't electric*.

Number 1. It isn't electric. Yes.

Guess What!

1

2

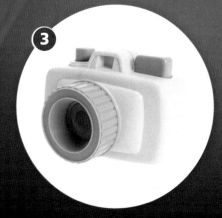

3

4

Project

4 Draw an electric toy.

→ Workbook page 26

Review Units 1 and 2

1 Look and say the word.   Number 1. Desk.

2 CD1 59 Listen and say the color.

Blue
What's this?
It's a (pencil case).

Red
Is it a (teddy bear)?
Yes, it is.
Is it an (art set)?
No, it isn't.

Finish

12

10

11

9

8

6

5

7

4

Yellow
How many books can you see?
I can see (six books).

1

2

3

Start

③ Family

Guess What!

1 (CD2 02) **Listen. Who's speaking?**

2 (CD2 03) **Listen, point, and say.**

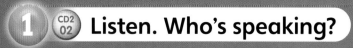 grandma

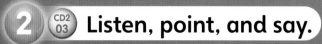 grandpa

3 dad

4 mom

5 uncle

6 aunt

7 brother

8 sister

9 cousin

3 (CD2 04) **Listen and find.**

Find Leo

4 CD2 05 **Say the chant.**

5 CD2 06 Think **Listen and say *yes* or *no*.** This is my dad. No!

→ Workbook page 31 Vocabulary **39**

6 CD2 08 **Sing the song.**

7 CD2 09 Think **Listen and say** *yes* **or** *no*.

→ Workbook page 32

8 CD2 10 **Listen, look, and say.**

1   **2**

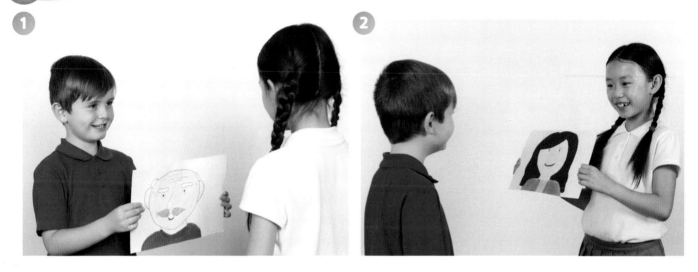

9 CD2 11 **Listen and say the color.**

10 About Me **Draw your family. Ask and answer.**

Who's this?   It's my brother. His name's Freddy.

Who's that? Is that your sister?   No, it isn't. It's my cousin.

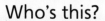

CD2 13 **Listen.**

ART SHOW

Value: Love your family

→ Workbook page 34

12   **Listen and act.**

Animal sounds

13 **Listen and say.**

A **dolphin** in a **red desk**.

What continent is it?

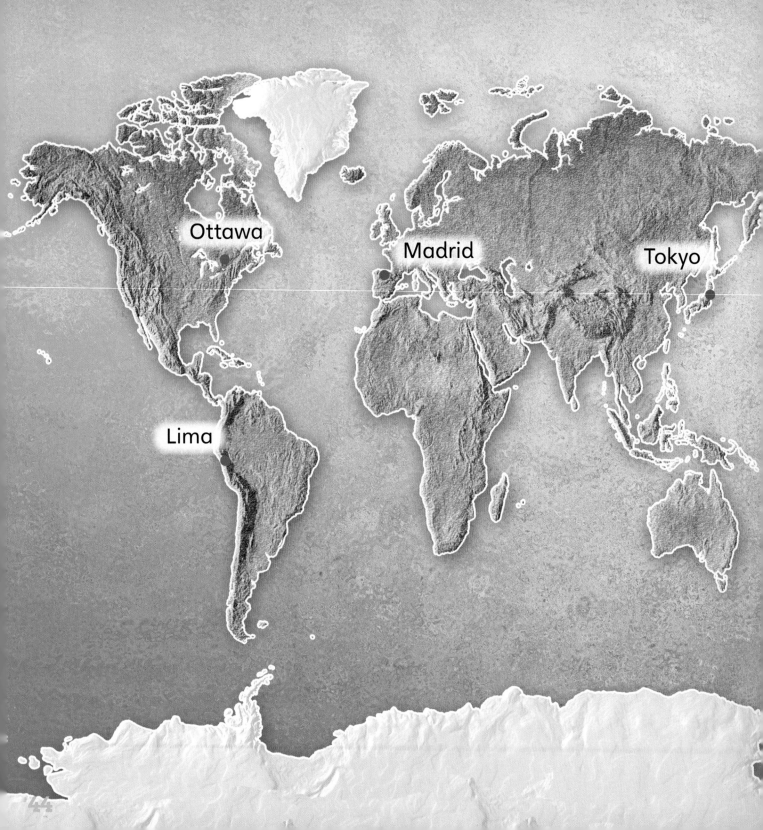

Ottawa

Madrid

Tokyo

Lima

1  **Listen and say.**

1. North America
2. South America
3. Europe
4. Africa
5. Asia
6. Australia
7. Antarctica

Guess What!

2 **Watch the video.**

3 **What continent are they from?**

My name's Akio. I'm from Tokyo.

My name's Zack. I'm from Ottawa.

My name's Luiz. I'm from Lima.

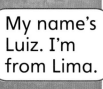

My name's Sofia. I'm from Madrid.

Project

4 **Color and stick the continents.**

→ Workbook page 36

4 At home

Guess What!

1 (CD2 21) **Listen. Who's speaking?**

2 (CD2 22) **Listen, point, and say.**

① house

② bathroom

③ bedroom

④ apartment

⑤ dining room

⑥ living room

⑦ balcony

⑧ kitchen

⑨ hallway

⑩ yard

Find Leo

3 (CD2 23) **Listen and find.**

4 CD2 24 **Say the chant.**

5 Think **Look and say the room.**   Number 1. Dining room.

6 CD2 26 **Listen, look, and say.**

1 2 3

7 CD2 27 **Listen and say**
Apartment 1 or **Apartment 2.**

Where's your Mom?　Apartment 2.

She's in the bedroom.

Apartment 1

Apartment 2

8 CD2 28 **Sing the song.**

9 CD2 29 **Listen and say *yes* or *no*.**

10 **Ask and answer.**

Where's the doll?

It's under the table.

Yes!

Grammar: *Where's the doll?* **51**

CD2 31 **Listen.**

①

② ⑤

③

④

⑤

⑥

Value: Take care of things

→ Workbook page 42

12 **Listen and act.**

Animal sounds

13 **Listen and say.**

An ant with an apple.

What shape is it?

1 (CD2 36) **Listen and say.**

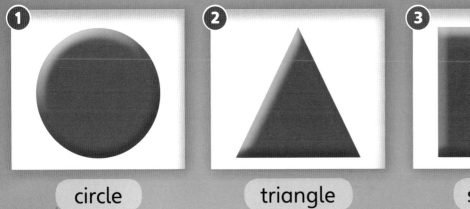

circle

triangle

square

2 Watch the video.

3 Look and say *circle*, *triangle*, or *square*.

What's this?   It's a circle!

Guess What!

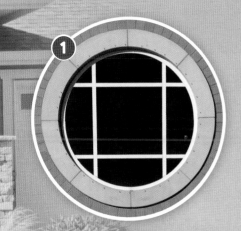

Project

4 Make a shapes picture.

Review Units 3 and 4

1 Look and say the words.   Number 1. Yard.

2 CD2 37 Listen and say the color.

→ Workbook pages 46–47

3 **Play the game.**

Yellow
Where's the (computer)?
It's (in) the (bedroom).

Orange
Where's your (grandma)?
(She) is in the (bedroom).

Start

Finish

My sounds

panda

bear

turtle

dolphin

ant

Workbook 1A
with Online Resources

Contents

Susan Rivers

Series Editor: Lesley Koustaff

CAMBRIDGE
UNIVERSITY PRESS

Hello!

1 **Look and match.**

a

b

c

d

2 **Ask and answer with a friend.**

1 Hello, I'm Mandy. What's your name?

2 Hello, I'm Jack.

3 This is Penny.

4 Hello, Penny.

Listen and stick.

4 CD1 08 **Listen and number.**

1

5 (Think) **What's next? Draw a line.**

① 2 4 6 2 4 6 2 4 ← 10
② 8 9 10 8 9 10 8 9 → 6
③ 3 5 7 3 5 7 3 5 4
④ 6 5 4 6 5 4 6 5 3
⑤ 1 8 3 1 8 3 1 8 7

6 (CD1 11) **Listen and write the numbers in the pictures.**

①

②

③

④

7 CD1 14 **Listen and color.**

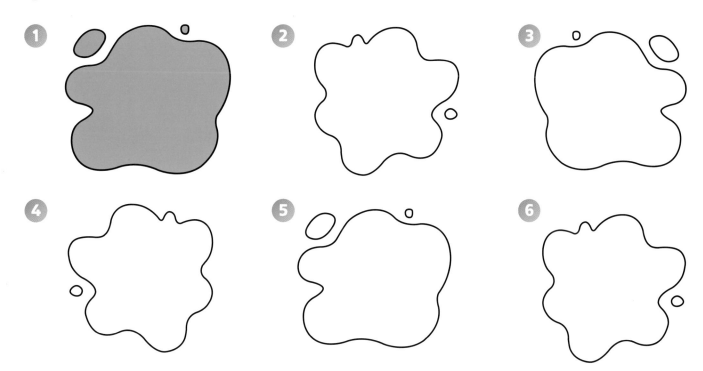

8 About Me **Look. Then draw and say.**

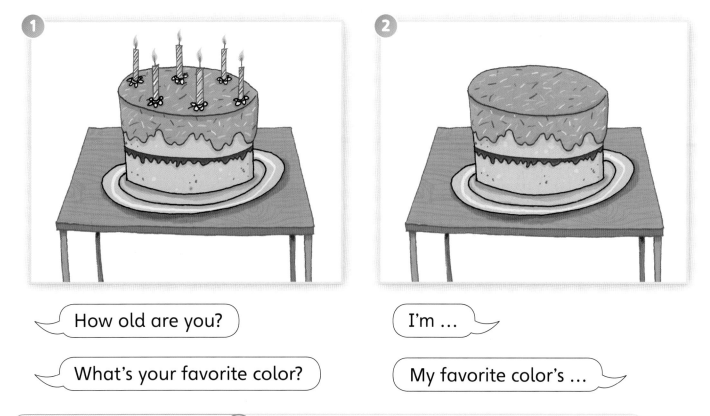

How old are you?

I'm …

What's your favorite color?

My favorite color's …

My picture dictionary → Go to page 48: Check the words you know and trace.

10 **What's missing? Look and draw. Then stick.**

I'm curious. ☺

11 **Trace the letters.**

A pink and
purple panda

12 CD1 19 **Listen and circle the *p* words.**

1
2
3
4

What color is it?

1 CD1 21 **Listen and color.**

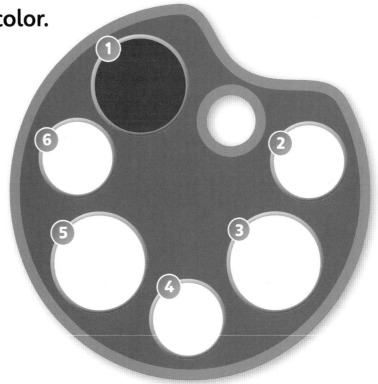

2 **Look and color.**

1  + =

2  + =

3  +  =

Evaluation

1 Follow the lines. Then trace and say.

a David

b Olivia

c Leo

d Tina

2 What's your favorite part? Use your stickers.

story   song   video

3 Puzzle Trace the color.

pink

Then go to page 55 and color the Hello! unit pieces.

11

1 CD1 25 **Listen and check ✓.**

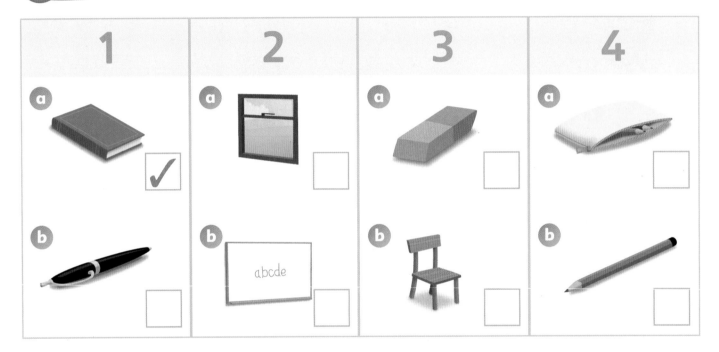

2 **Look and match.**

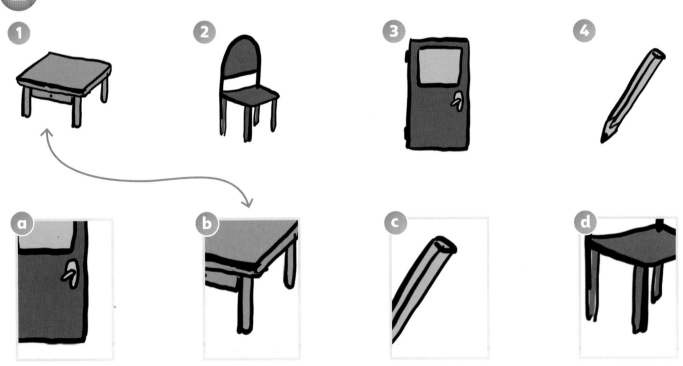

3 CD1 27 Listen and stick.

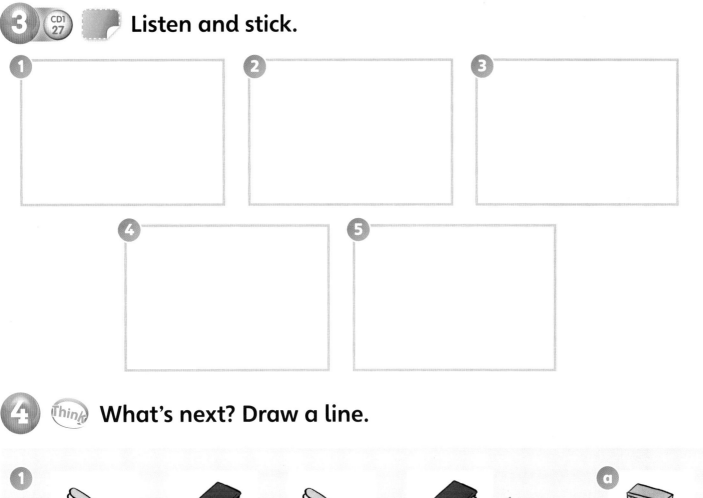

4 Think What's next? Draw a line.

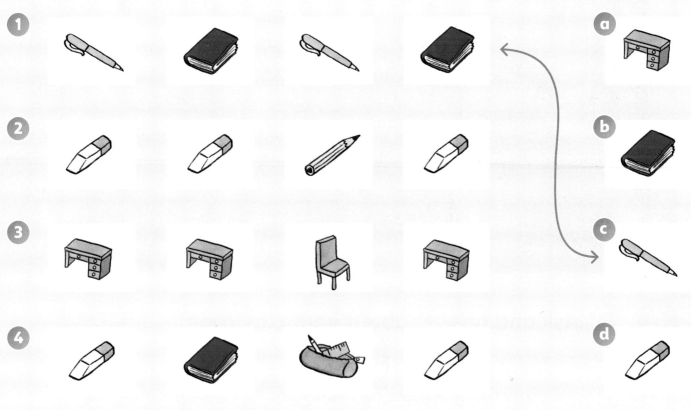

My picture dictionary → Go to page 49: Check the words you know and trace.

5 Look and count. Write the number.

2

6 (About Me) Ask and answer about your classroom.

How many erasers can you see? | Three.

7 CD1 32 Listen and check ✓ or put an ✗.

1  ✗

2

3

4

8 Think Circle the different one.

1 a  b  c  d

2 a b  c d

Grammar **15**

9 CD1 34 **Listen, look, and match.**

10 **What's missing? Look and draw. Then stick.**

I'm friendly.

11 **Trace the letters.**

A bear with
a blue book.

12 CD1 37 **Listen and circle the *b* words.**

What material is it?

1 Look and match.

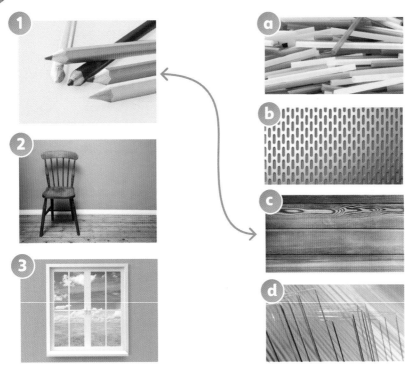

2 CD1 39 Listen and check ✓.

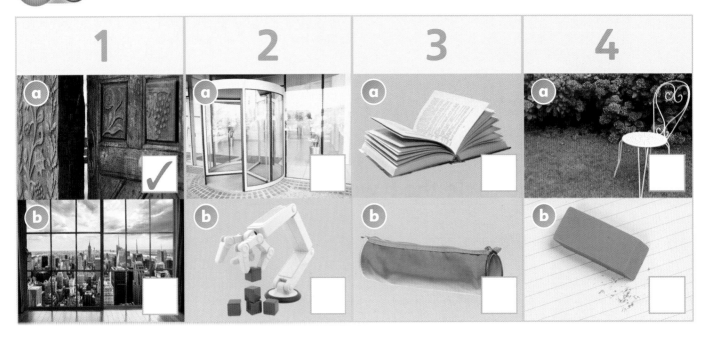

Evaluation

1 **Look and trace. Then say.**

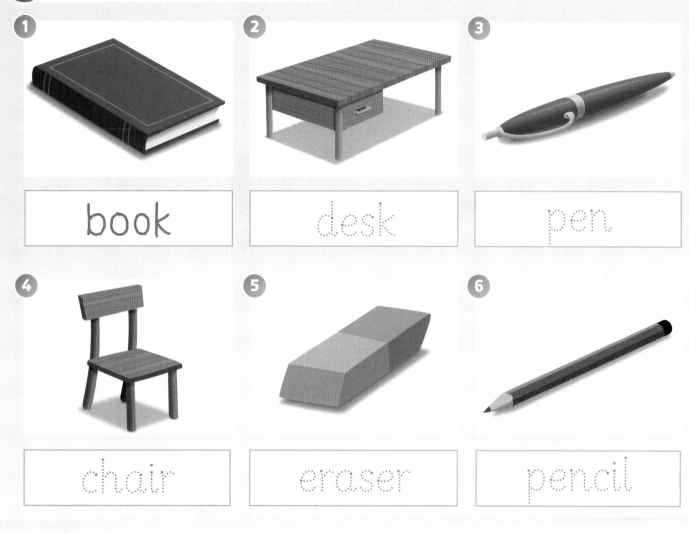

book   desk   pen

chair   eraser   pencil

2 What's your favorite part?
Use your stickers.

story   song   video

3 Puzzle Trace the color.

red

Then go to page
55 and color
the Unit 1 pieces.

19

2 Toys

1 CD1 43 **Listen and check ✓.**

	1	2	3	4
a	✓			
b				

2 **Look, match, and say.**   1 kite.

3  CD1 45 **Listen and stick.**

① ② ③

④ ⑤

4 Think **Look and circle the toys.**

My picture dictionary → Go to page 50: Check the words you know and trace.

5 (CD1 48) **Listen and check ✓ or put an ✗.**

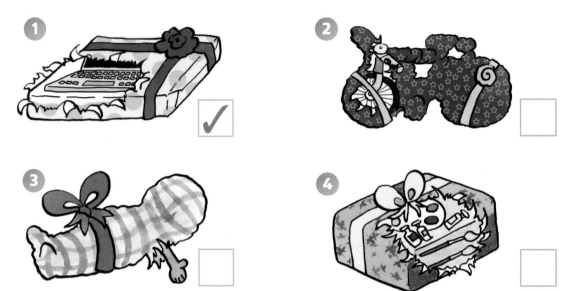

1. ✓
2. ☐
3. ☐
4. ☐

6 (About Me) **Draw your favorite toy and say.**

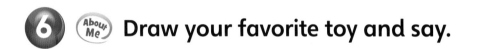

What's this?

It's a ...

7 **Listen and number the pictures.**

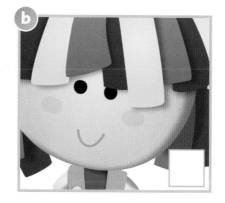

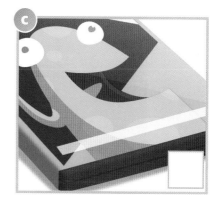

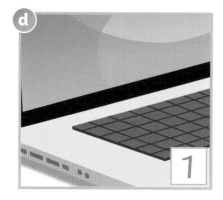

1

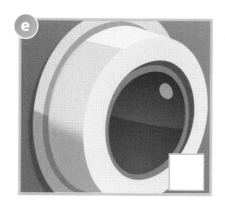

8 **Listen and draw the pictures.**

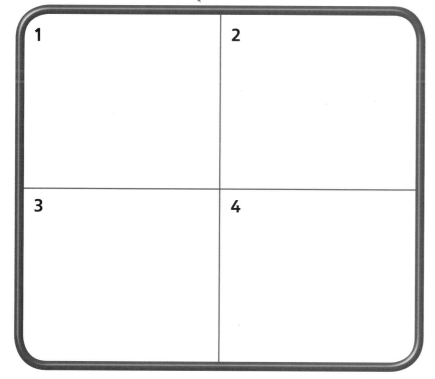

1

2

3

4

Listen and check ✓.

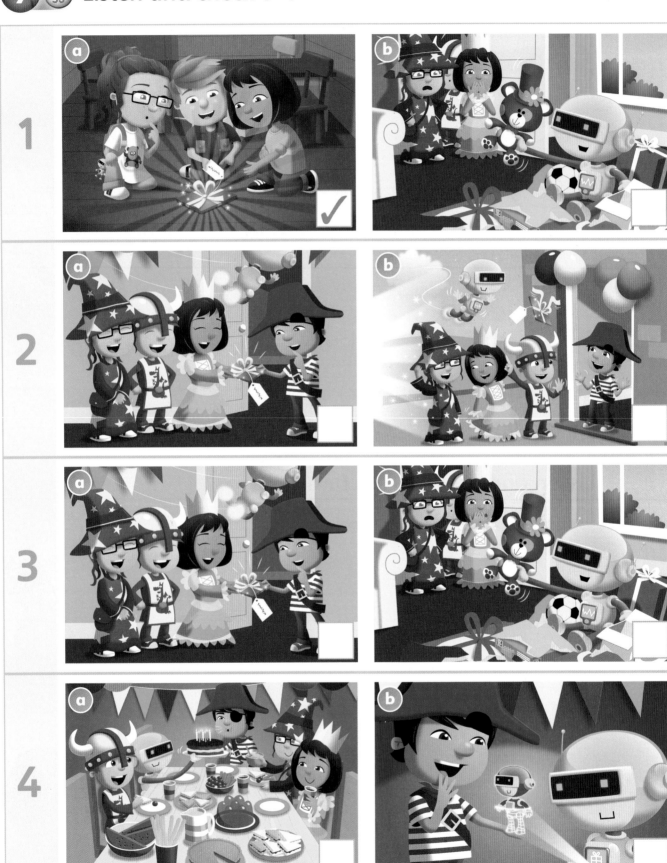

10 **What's missing? Look and draw. Then stick.**

I'm polite.

11 **Trace the letters.**

A turtle with two teddy bears.

12 **Listen and circle the *t* words.**

Is it electric?

1 **CD1 58** Listen and check ✓ (electric) or put an ✗ (not electric).

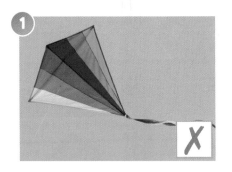 1 ✗

 2

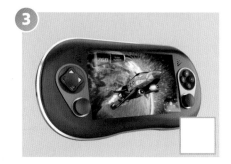 3

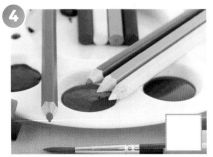 4

 5

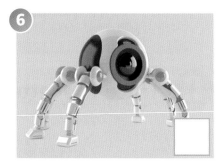 6

2 Look at Activity 1 and draw.

Electric   Not electric

Evaluation

1 **Look and trace. Then say.**

1
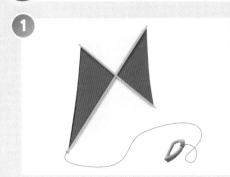
kite

2

robot

3

ball

4

bike

5

doll

6

camera

2  **What's your favorite part? Use your stickers.**

story   song   video

3 **Puzzle** **Trace the color.**

green

Then go to page 55 and color the Unit 2 pieces.

Review Units 1 and 2

1 Look and say. Find and circle.

Listen and number the pictures.

a

b

c

d

1

e

f

7

Family

1 **Trace the words and match.**

1 mom

2 dad

3 sister

4 brother

5 grandma

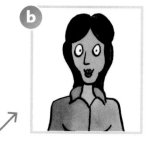

2 **Look and write the number.**

1 cousin   2 uncle   3 grandpa   4 aunt

3 CD2 07 Listen and stick.

1   2   3   4   5

4 Think Read, look, and check ✓.

1 dad

☐ ☐ ✓

2 aunt

☐ ☐ ☐

3 grandma

☐ ☐ ☐

4 brother

☐ ☐ ☐

My picture dictionary → Go to page 51: Check the words you know and trace.

5 Look, read, and match.

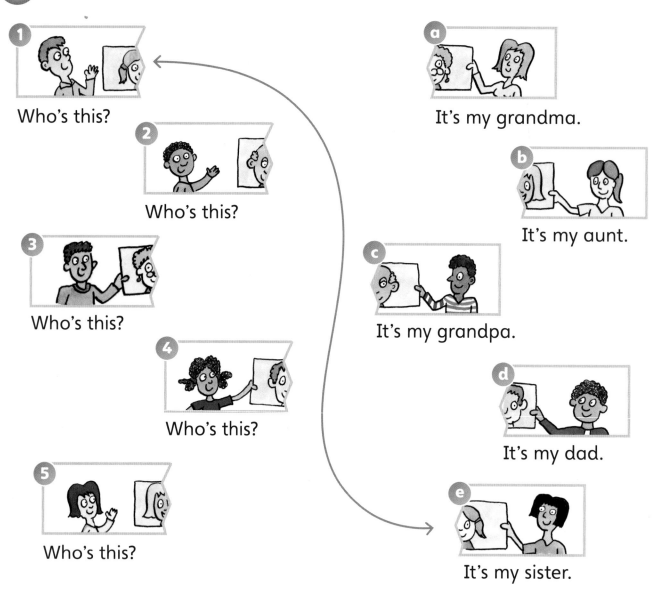

1 Who's this?

2 Who's this?

3 Who's this?

4 Who's this?

5 Who's this?

a It's my grandma.

b It's my aunt.

c It's my grandpa.

d It's my dad.

e It's my sister.

6 (About Me) Draw a member of your family. Then ask and answer with a friend.

Who's this?

It's my ... .

7 **Listen, read, and check ✓.**

1

my brother ☐

my cousin ✓

2

my mom ☐

my aunt ☐

3

my mom ☐

my grandma ☐

4

my sister ☐

my cousin ☐

5

my cousin ☐

my aunt ☐

6

my dad ☐

my uncle ☐

8 **Look, read, and circle the correct word.**

1 Who's **this** / (**that**)?
It's my uncle.

2 Who's **this** / **that**?
It's my cousin.

3 Who's **this** / **that**?
It's my grandpa.

4 Who's **this** / **that**?
It's my sister.

9 Listen, look, and match.

10 **What's missing? Look and draw. Then stick.**

I love my family.

11 **Trace the letters.**

A dolphin in a red desk.

12 **Listen and circle the _d_ words.**

1    2    3    4

What continent is it?

 Listen and write the number.

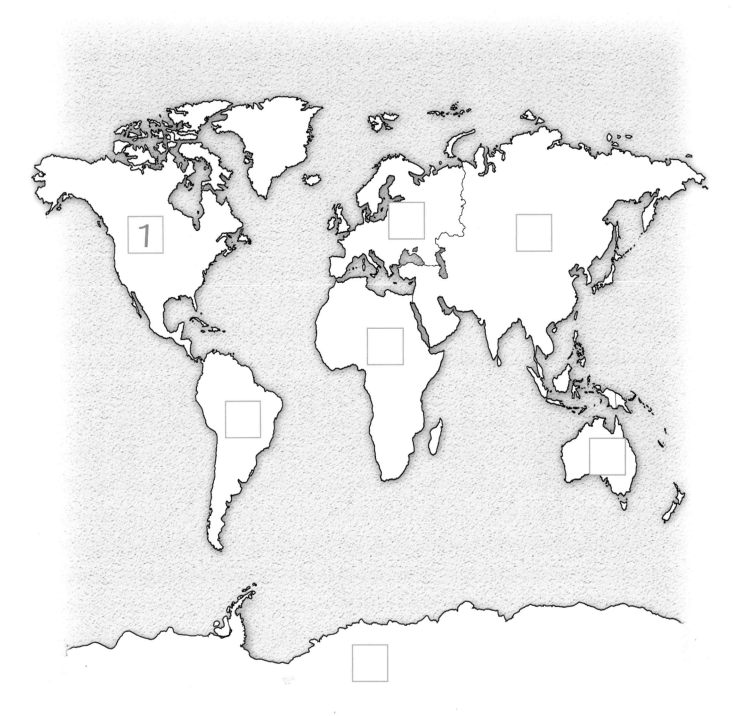

 Look at the map again. Listen and color.

Evaluation

1 Read and trace. Then circle and say.

1 aunt

a b

2 grandma

a b

3 uncle

a b

4 brother

a b

2 What's your favorite part? Use your stickers.

story   song   video

3 Puzzle Complete the color.

o_a_g_

Then go to page 55 and color the Unit 3 pieces.

4 At home

1 Look at the picture and write the letter.

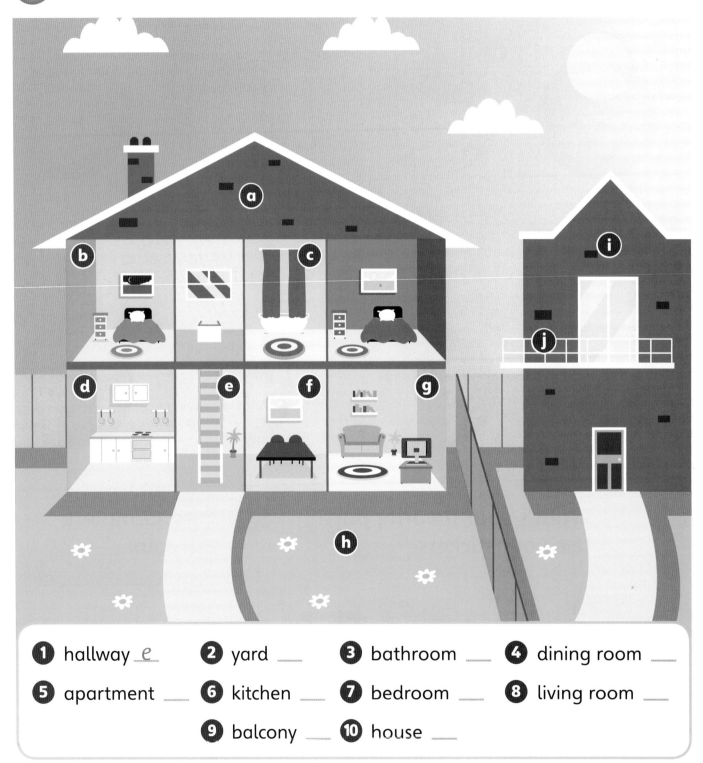

1 hallway _e_ **2** yard ___ **3** bathroom ___ **4** dining room ___

5 apartment ___ **6** kitchen ___ **7** bedroom ___ **8** living room ___

9 balcony ___ **10** house ___

2  **Listen and stick.**

1	2	3

4	5	6

3 **Look, read, and circle the correct word.**

1 (kitchen) / dining room

2 hallway / living room

3 bedroom / balcony

4 kitchen / bathroom

5 hallway / yard

6 balcony / dining room

My picture dictionary Go to page 52: Check the words you know and trace.

Look, read, and match.

1
Where's your aunt?

2
Where's your cousin?

3
Where's your mom?

4
Where are you?

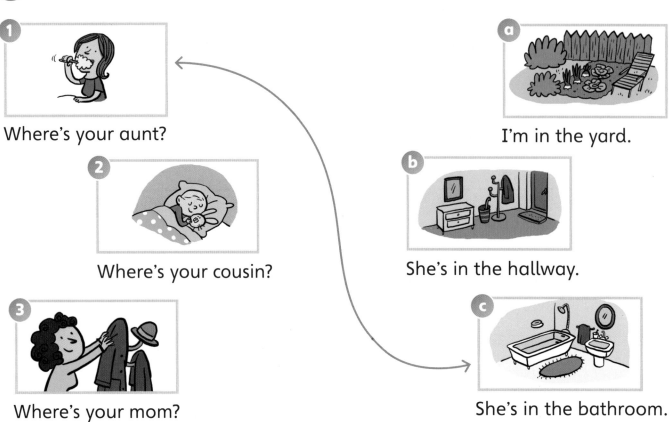

a
I'm in the yard.

b
She's in the hallway.

c
She's in the bathroom.

d
He's in the bedroom.

5 **Draw yourself. Ask and answer with a friend.**

Where are you?

I'm in ...

6 **Listen and write the number.**

1   2  3 4  5

7 **Draw the objects in the picture. Ask and answer.**

Where's the ... ?   It's ... .

Grammar **41**

8 CD2 32 Listen and number.

9 **What's missing? Look and draw. Then stick.**

I take care of things.

a

b

c

10 **Trace the letters.**

An ant with an apple.

11 CD2 35 **Listen and circle the *a* words.**

1

2

3

4

What shape is it?

1 Look and color the shapes.

2 What's next? Match, then draw and color the shapes.

square

1. ▲ ● ▲ ● ▲

triangle

2. ■ ■ ● ● ■

circle

3. ● ■ ▲ ● ■

Evaluation

1 Read and trace. Then circle and say.

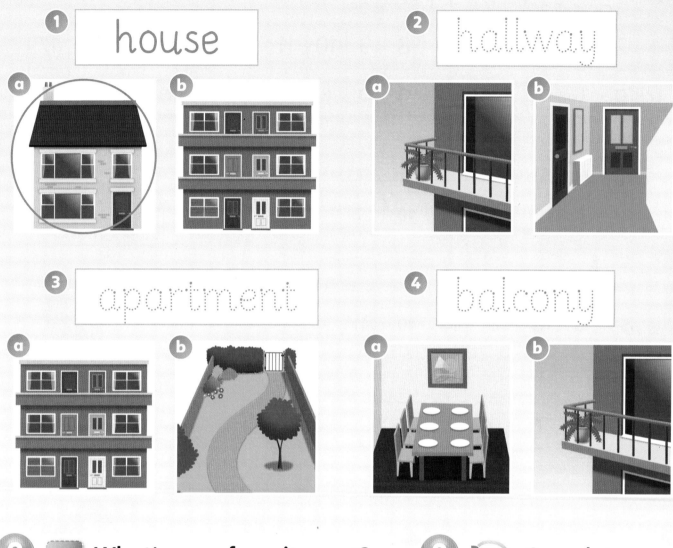

1 house

2 hallway

3 apartment

4 balcony

2 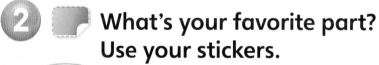 What's your favorite part? Use your stickers.

story   song   video

3 Puzzle Complete the color.

y_l_o_

Then go to page 55 and color the Unit 4 pieces.

Review Units 3 and 4

1 Write the words and match.

1	2	3	4	5	6	7	8	9	10	11	12	13	14	15	16	17
u	a	t	b	s	c	r	d	o	e	n	g	m	h	k	i	y

1

b   r   o   t   h   e   r

4   7   9   3   14   10   7

2

___ ___ ___ ___ ___ ___ ___

15   16   3   6   14   10   11

3

___ ___ ___ ___ ___ ___ ___

12   7   2   11   8   13   2

4

___ ___ ___ ___

17   2   7   8

5

___ ___ ___

8   2   8

6

___ ___ ___ ___ ___

14   9   1   5   10

a

b

c

d

e

f

46

2 **Read and match the questions with the answers.**

1 Where's the computer? _c_   **a** She's in the living room.
2 Is that your cousin? ___   **b** No, it isn't. It's my sister.
3 Who's that? ___   **c** It's on the desk.
4 Where's your mom? ___   **d** It's my sister.

3 **Circle the correct words and write.**

mom   bedroom   grandma   ~~under~~

1

What's / (Where's) the doll?
It's _under_ the bed.

2

Who's / Where's this?
It's my _____ .

3

Who / Where are you?
I'm in my _____ .

4

Is that / Who's your aunt?
No, it isn't.
It's my _____ .

Hello!

blue ☐

green ☐

orange ☐

pink ☐

purple ☐

red ☐

yellow ☐

1 School

board

book

chair

desk

door

pen

pencil

pencil case

eraser

window

2 Toys

☐
art set

☐
ball

☐
bike

☐
camera

☐
computer

☐
computer game

☐
doll

☐
kite

☐
robot

☐
teddy bear

3 Family

aunt ☐

brother ☐

cousin ☐

dad ☐

grandma ☐

grandpa ☐

mom ☐

sister ☐

uncle ☐

4 At home

balcony

bathroom

bedroom

dining room

apartment

yard

hallway

house

kitchen

living room

My puzzle

Thanks and Acknowledgements

Many thanks to everyone in the excellent team at Cambridge University Press. In particular we would like to thank Emily Hird, Liane Grainger, Camilla Agnew, and Flavia Lamborghini whose professionalism, enthusiasm, experience, and talent makes them all such a pleasure to work with.

We would also like to give special thanks to Lesley Koustaff for her unfailing support, expert guidance, good humor, and welcome encouragement throughout the project.

The authors and publishers would like to thank the following contributors:

Blooberry Design: concept design, cover design, book design, page makeup

Emma Szlachta, Vicky Bewick: editing

Lisa Hutchins: freelance editing

Ann Thomson: art direction, picture research

Gareth Boden: commissioned photography

Jon Barlow: commissioned photography

Ian Harker: audio recording

Robert Lee, Dib Dib Dub Studios: song and chant composition

Vince Cross: theme tune composition

James Richardson: arrangement of theme tune

John Marshall Media: audio recording and production

Phaebus: video production

hyphen S.A.: publishing management, American English edition

The authors and publishers acknowledge the following sources of copyright material and are grateful for the permissions granted. Although every effort has been made, it has not always been possible to identify the sources of all the material used, or to trace all copyright holders.

If any omissions are brought to our notice, we will be happy to include the appropriate acknowledgments on reprinting.

The authors and publishers would like to thank the following illustrators:

Student's Book
Bill Bolton: pp 28; Chris Jevons (Bright Agency): pp 18, 50; Joelle Dreidemy (Bright Agency): pp 17, 27, 49; Kirsten Collier (Bright Agency): pp 11, 21, 31, 43, 53, 58; Marcus Cutler (Sylvie Poggio): pp 35, 57; Marek Jagucki: pp 5, 6, 9, 10, 15, 16, 20, 25, 26, 30, 37, 38, 39, 42, 47, 48, 52, 56; Mark Duffin: pp 13, 44; Richard Watson (Bright Agency): pp 41, 50; Woody Fox (Bright Agency): pp 18, 29, 40, 51

Workbook
Marek Jagucki p4, 5, 8, 11, 12, 16, 17, 19, 20, 23, 24, 27, 34, 35, 37, 42, 45, 55, stickers; Joelle Dreidemy (Bright Agency) p6, 9, 12, 15, 29, 31, 33, 40, 47; Woody Fox (Bright Agency) p13, 21, 22, 30, 32, 39, 41, 43, 46, stickers; Sarah Jennings (Bright Agency) p7, 9, 13, 15, 17, 20, 21, 23, 25, 35, 39, 43, stickers; Chris Jevons (Bright Agency) p14, 28, 33, 38, 41; Marcus Cutler (Sylvie Poggio) p37; Mark Duffin p10, 36, 44; Hardinge (Monkey Feet) p48, 49, 50, 51, 52

The authors and publishers would like to thank the following for permission to reproduce photographs:

Student's Book
p.2–3: holbox/Shutterstock; p.4–5: SAMSUL SAID/Reuters/Corbis; p.6 (CL): Fertnig/Getty Images; p.6 (C): Margot Hartford/Alamy; p.6 (CR): Blend Images/ Alamy; p.11 (B/G), p.21 (B/G): SZE FEI WONG/Getty Images; p.11 (T): Mike Kemp/Getty Images; p.12–13 (B/G):plusphoto/Getty Images; p.13 (C): TongoRo Images/Alamy; p.13 (BL): Leigh Prather/Shutterstock; p.13 (BC): Valery Voennyy/Alamy; p.14–15: Pat Canova/Alamy; p.17 (TL): UltraONEs/Getty Images; p.17 (TC): Kimberly Hosey/Getty Images; p.17 (TR): MiguelMalo/Getty Images; p.17 (CL): Vincent St. Thomas/shutterstock; p.17 (C): Picsfive/Shutterstock; p.17 (CR): Dimitris66/Getty Images; p.22–23: VisitBritain/Pawel Libera/Getty Images; p.23 (T-1): Shutterstock/My Life Graphic; p.23 (T-2): Shutterstock/ Vorobyeva; p.23 (T-3): Jesus Keller/ Shutterstock; p.23 (T-4): Foonia/Shutterstock, p.23 (B-1): Shutterstock/ ETIENjones, p.23 (B-2): bikeriderlondon/Shutterstock; p.23 (B-3): Jerome Skiba/Getty Images; p.23 (B-4): hayatikayhan/Getty Images; p.24–25: Zhang Chunlei/Xinhua Press/Corbis; p.27 (TL): stable/Shutterstock; p.27 (TC): Chesky/Shutterstock; p.27 (TR): ONOKY-Photononstop/Alamy; p.31 (B/G), p.43 (B/G): Jolanta Wojcicka/Shutterstock; p.32–33: Shutterstock/ Anna Rubak; p.33 (TL): ffolas/Shutterstock; p.33 (TC): Prapann/Shutterstock; p.33 (TR): meKCar/Shutterstock; p.33 (CL): Shutterstock/Sergiy Kuzmin; p.33 (C): Shutterstock/Ociacia; p.33 (BL): Shutterstock/HomeStudio; p.33 (BC): Shutterstock/ Chiyacat; p.34 (1): Shutterstock/archideaphoto; p.34 (2): Shutterstock/Picsfive; p.34 (3): Shutterstock/Ingvar Bjork; p.34 (4): sunsetman/Shutterstock; p.34 (5): Shutterstock/Jojje; p.34 (6): Shutterstock/ Lim Yong Hian; p.34 (7): Shutterstock/ Craig Jewell; p.34 (8): Shutterstock/ Sergii Figurnyi; p.34 (CL): SuperStock/Tetra Images; p.34 (CR), p.34 (BL): Alamy/MBI; p.34 (BR): SuperStock/AsiaPix; p.36–37: JACQUES Pierre/ hemis.fr/Getty Images; p.39 (TL): Blend Images/Alamy; p.39 (TC): Shotshop GmbH/Alamy; p.39 (TR): Shutterstock/Monkey Business Images; p.45 (TL): Ekkaruk Dongpuyow/Alamy; p.45 (CL): mamahoohooba/Alamy; p.45 (CR): Cultura RM/Alamy; p.45 (BL): Keith Levit/Alamy; p.45 (BC): Rick Gomez/ Getty Images; p.46–47: Vaughn Greg/Getty Images; p.49 (TL): Simon Montgomery/ Getty Images; p.49 (TR): Compassionate Eye Foundation/ Rob Daly/ OJO Images Ltd/ Getty Images; p.49 (CL): DEA/G. DAGLI ORTI/ Getty Images; p.49 (CR): Chuck Schmidt/Getty Images; p.53 (B/G): Tim Jackson/Getty Images; p.53 (T): Radius Images/Alamy; p.54–55: romakoma/ Shutterstock, p.55 (1): RDFlemming/ Shutterstock; p.55 (2): Alamy/Andrew Holt; p.55 (3): Shotshop GmbH/Alamy; p.55 (4): Alamy/Ros Drinkwater; p.56 (1): Mark Boulton/Alamy; p.56 (3): Shotshop GmbH/Alamy; p.56 (5): Breadmaker/Shutterstock; p.56 (7): Aardvark/Alamy; p.56 (CL): Alamy/ Westend61 GmbH; p.56 (CR): Shutterstock/Flashon Studio; p.56 (BL): MBI/ Alamy; p.56 (BR): Alamy/Richard Newton.

Commissioned photography by Gareth Boden: p.13 (BR), p.23 (BR), p.33 (BR), p.45 (BR), p.55 (BR); Jon Barlow: p.7, p.19, p.21 (T), p.28, p.29 (B), p.31 (T), p.41, p.43 (T), p.51 (B)

Workbook
p. 4 (unit header): © SAMSUL SAID/Reuters/Corbis; p. 10 (header): plusphoto/Shutterstock; p. 12 (unit header): © Pat Canova / Alamy; p. 18 (header): VisitBritain/Pawel Libera/Getty Images; p. 18 (Ex 1: photo 1): pixsfile/Getty Images; p. 18 (Ex: photo 2): Julian James Ward/Getty Images; p. 18 (Ex: photo 3): Peshkova/Getty Images; p. 18 (Ex: photo a): myibean/ Getty Images; p. 18 (Ex: photo b): ULTRA.F/Getty Images; p. 18 (Ex: photo c): sorendls/Getty Images; p. 18 (Ex: photo d): © BonkersAboutPictures/ Alamy; p. 18 (Ex: photo 4): Nokz/Shutterstock; p. 18 (Ex: photo 5): Spiderstock/Getty Images; p. 18 (Ex: photo 6): Zoonar RF/Getty Images; p. 18 (Ex 2: photo 1a): Ocskay Bence/Shutterstock; p. 18 (Ex 2: photo 1b): stockelements/Shutterstock; p. 18 (Ex 2: photo 2a): Martin Barraud/Getty Images; p. 18 (Ex 2: photo 2b): Alexander Bedrin/Getty Images; p. 18 (Ex 2: photo 3a): pedrosala/Shutterstock; p. 18 (Ex 2: photo 3b): Robert Babczynski/Shutterstock; p. 18 (Ex 2: photo 4a): pedrosala/Shutterstock; p. 18 (Ex 2: photo 4b): photastic/Shutterstock; p. 20 (unit header): © Zhang Chunlei/Xinhua Press/Corbis; p. 26 (header): Anna RubaK/Shutterstock; p. 26 (photo 1): ElementalImaging/Getty Images; p. 26 (photo 2): longoria-td/Getty Images; p. 26 (photo 3): Baris Simsek/Getty Images; p. 26 (photo 4): peangdao/Getty Images; p. 26 (photo 5): Lisa Valder/Getty Images; p. 26 (photo 6): Talaj/Getty Images; p. 30 (unit header): JACQUES Pierre/ hemis.fr/Getty Images; p. 36 (header): © Ekkaruk Dongpuyow/Alamy; p. 38 (unit header): Vaughn Greg/Getty Images; p. 44 (header): romakoma/ Shutterstock.

Our special thanks to the following for their kind help during location photography:

Radmore Farm Shop, Queen Emma primary School

Front Cover photo by **Premium/UIG/Getty Images**

Front Cover illustration by **Premium/UIG/Getty Images**

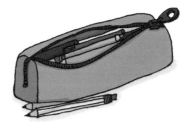

  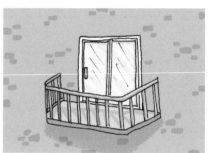